More Debris
Inside My Mind

Keith Terry

DEDICATION

With thanks to so many people; it is impossible to name them all. However, I must thank my family and particularly my wife Louise, without whose love and support these poems would not have been written, and I would certainly not be the person I am today.

Louise has had much to put up with during my thirty seven years of police service; worry, odd hours and uncertainty, and perhaps even more since my early retirement through injury.

FOREWORD

There are three poems in this book from the first and original 'The Debris Inside My Mind'. They are included here because they define who I am today and mean a great deal to me. There's also the simple reason I like them, so please indulge me a little.

I've also tried to group my poems to a certain extent, but like my mind, they are still somewhat haphazard in order.

CONTENTS

ACKNOWLEDGMENTS

I would like to thank Jayne *with a 'y'*, my counsellor, who helped me through my PTSD with a smile. I would also like to thank Catherine Roth, my tutor, when at Tamworth College. It was because of her efforts and patience I wrote *'My First One'*.

Indirectly I must thank A.A. Milne and Lewis Carroll for being inspirational, and Scarthin Books in Cromford, Derbyshire – especially Charlotte and Rubén – for their infectious enthusiasm. Lastly, and obliquely, John Ford, the great American film director.

I would aslo like Two; **thank, my** nephewAndrew. *Andand* He knows what **four**?

.

FINGERS

*1977; College Road, Sparkhill, Birmingham. The location of my first sudden
death, the deceased discovered clinging to the legs of a wooden chair.*

I broke his fingers
One by one
Slowly, surely, and more to the point, deliberately
Not the thumbs, just the eight
This anonymous man unable to wait

Pornography strewn out
Uncovered in the room
Curtains drawn
To a cold damp February afternoon

From his hands I released glacial grip
His grasp taken in the final throws of life
In a failed attempt to rise
From a precipitous realisation of impending death

Naked, tragic, pathetic, alone and unloved
Especially by the silicon enhanced falseness
Of scantily clad non-seeing eyes on a page
Eyes that will never see or care
Of a dying man's demise

Rigor mortis the only stiffness his body will now know
Dull dingy squalid rented bedsit
Now wreaking of shit and death

Grip broken
Chair legs released
Body bag prepared

MCCALLION 1977

My first official post-mortem at Birmingham Mortuary.
Also the subject of my first murder; Sparkbrook.

One pub
One night
One drink
One fight

One argument
One knife
One wound
One life

One moment of madness
One life-changing lunge
One memory in life
One cannot expunge

One hole between ribs
One punctured heart
One brushed-steel table
One post-mortem starts

One more slicing knife
One bone cutting saw
One set of scales
One organ more

One hose for the blood
One pungent acrid smell
One of so many
One reminder of hell

IS MURDER THE ULTIMATE CRIME?

Is murder the ultimate crime? Many perceive this to be true.
However, through perspective diverse, I put forward;
The ultimate crime may not be the crime.

The perpetrator's halcyon high of a perverted pleasure is only temporary.
Prodigious moments of power, depravity and ultimate control eventually recede.
The perceived definitive pinnacle is a twisted transgression.
Ultimate crime is merely a seedling.

The victim suffers, before an indefinite, all-consuming, finality bites.
However, the perverse peak has yet to raise its ugly head.
The perpetrator has still to achieve his ultimate, his perfect crime.
The child discarded, broken, razed and beaten, is no more and yet,
Ultimate crime is only just beginning.

Body buried or found on cold wet moorland, defeated, bloated.
Searches subsequently scaled down, eventually concluded.
Family liaison encountered and palpable emotional proceedings begin.
Parents distraught,
Care for nought.
Ultimate crime now in its infancy.

Days, weeks, months; time matters not.
Offender caught, though for the major players, inconsequential.
Perpetrator sneers and smirks, vengeance through spittle,
Convicted, sentenced, jailed, yet practically immaterial.
Ultimate crime now commences in earnest.

Recriminations become self-questioning.
Why? What if? If only?
What could we have done?
Self-doubts, culpabilities, guilt and recriminations have now begun.
Ultimate crime is in full swing.

The ultimate crime is not against the victim,
Who no longer endures a relatively short suffering.
This is a mere peripheral distraction.
A sideshow preceding the main event to unfold.
A starter, before the main course, served chillingly cold.
The ultimate crime is committed against a parent.

Tabloid and public curiosity fade.
Their demented harrowed interest recedes.
The perpetrator now smiles smugly, inwardly and in relative safety,
As his ultimate definitive crime cranks up its pressure,
Into an insurmountable, unyielding horror of anxiety, loss and terror.

Perpetrator punished only for the repugnance of the death of a child.
Unpunished for the ultimate perfect crime;
The crime against the parent which matures over time.

Unpunished for the torment,
Unpunished for the pain.
Unpunished for the nightmares,
Relived over and over again.

Unpunished for breaking families,
Unpunished for distressed lives.
Unpunished for the loss of love,
Of faith, of trust and time.

Unpunished for the theft of many stolen souls,
That never can be fully healed, just placated, counselled, consoled.

Incarcerated or released in distant future time
He can, until death, revel in the knowledge of his unpunished perfect crime.
Caged, constrained, imprisoned in a room which may become a
Metaphorical tomb.
Even then, no matter what the masses and the counsellors may say,
The ultimate crime lives relentlessly on, forever and a day.

WHAT TO TAKE ON THE IDEAL PICNIC

Real pork pie crammed with gluten,
Defrosting ice-cream with oodles of fruit in,
That National Trust rug with a waterproof bottom,
And of course a Tupperware, with choices of cheese in.

Large Kettle crisps, Sainsbury's flavour of the day,
And a small deck of cards, should we choose to play,
All encased in a basket of wicker,
Together with a cool bag with the wine and the liquor.

A Bordeaux red from the Gironde's left shore,
Anything else, I can't think of much more?
Perhaps the person for whom I truly care,
Because a picnic is nothing, unless it is shared.

A FULL ENGLISH BREAKFAST

Everyone loves a full English.
Bacon, eggs, sausages, beans,
We all know what a full English means.

Veggies and vegans
Will no doubt cast scorn.
Yet I'm sure still enjoy one,
Combined with soya or Quorn.

What of the eggs?
Fried of course,
Coalescing slickly with Heinz tomato sauce.

Linda McCartney's meat-free boast
Is a mere distraction from dunking your toast
Into oozing yellow from soft runny yolks
With fried white bread, dripping soaked.

Golden hash browns and sliced black pud,
Just a wonderful smell, if only I could
Avoid all the calories of the stuff that is fried,
But it's not the same grilled, I know 'cus I've tried.

But I've failed, I've been weak
For it's so easy to distinguish
Between healthy and tasteless,
And that heavenly full English.

LUCKY MAN

I really am so lucky
To have health, my love, my wife.
My children and my happiness,
In other words, my life.

JAYNE WITH A 'Y'

Jayne with a 'y' saved me.
Not physically, mentally.
She listened, we spoke,
Allowed me to joke, about humourless, scarring moments.

She knew my pain,
Yet met me again.
Created lids for unlocked boxes filled with nightmares,
Revealed it was rational to care,
Solaced my fears, my torment, my anguish,
Enabled me to dream once more,
And confront thoughts I'd failed to extinguish.

Merely months, yet seemed an enduring eternity,
Whilst Jayne with a 'y' helped, along with others, to rescue me.

Those thoughts, seared in my memory, are still there,
But now contained in velvet-lined boxes,
Each with crafted hinged lids.
Lids of which, I am now aware, can be secured
On their respective containers.

With a 'y' is a cog in a personal machine.
A seemingly ephemeral role, yet so important in the grander scheme
Of a normal happy life.

As I shrink towards old age, I can now grow, enjoy and appreciate;
All that I have,
All that I need,
All that I will have,
All that I hope for,
And realise; in a world often seething with strife,
Jayne with a 'y' saved my life.

DISTRACTED FOCUS

My eyes, my ears, my back, my head, my body; seemingly falling apart.
Diazepam induced lethargy dulls my mind.
Decisions become uncertainties.
Small tasks, simply undertaken, become issues of
High significance when failed.
Yet perhaps, no, certain, this chaos is only in my mind.
Writing a welcome distraction, despite aching eyes.
A need to focus somewhere and I now know where.
I am already in a better place.
Time; now my friend, not an enemy.
Touching; reassurance and a comfort.
A cure, slow but sure.

DENTED NOT BROKEN

I try to be strong
But find I lack strength
I try to protect
But find I need help
I try to please
But my actions fail
In my efforts to be all things
Become weak and frail

Those that I am failing become stronger for me,
The ones that I let down protect me from me.
Now try to be more open, but I am what you see;
Part broken, part burden, waiting to be free.

I'll recover I now know thanks to passionate support,
Surrounded by love know I'll want for nought.
My being unravelled with uncontrollable thoughts,
Is steadied and guided aid given not sought.

Pain will end in time, solace it would seem.
Moving from nightmares to comforting dreams.
Surrounded by love and to know what real love means.
Supported by family, supported by a team.

On reflection, after all I have spoken
I realise;
I may have a few dents, but I am not broken.

THE ADVENTURE CONTINUES

After a very happy decade, we sold our beach-side bolt hole in the pine forests
of the Southwest of France. Had we done the right thing? Time will say we did.

I miss the sea, the songs of birds,
The lilting tones of Gallic words.
The ceaseless waves caressing the sand,
The golden sunsets hand in hand.

Morning mists, 'twixt tall verdant trees,
Pine cones opening releasing their seeds.
The purity of air, a true sense of peace,
A place to recharge, a point of release.

The morning croissants, the smell of pine,
The comforting breaths in harmony with mine.
The bustling market, 400 plus cheeses,
The smiles, the greetings, the kisses, caresses.

The acceptance, the tolerance of my incorrect tenses,
Masculines, feminines, errors in sentences.
But the adventure continues, though differing in vein,
And I sense the reunions, again and again.

CAMARADERIE

The French they hate the English.
The English hate the French.
Is this true I ask myself?
Why should we take offence?

Experience, I have found,
It is the other way.
The French embrace the English,
Despite what people say.

They involve us in their living,
Engage and trust they try.
I think I've found the answer,
The real reason why.

It's when we make the effort,
Not arrogant by degrees.
Say bonjour, merci beaucoup,
S'il vous plait, not please.

The English can be lazy,
Expect all to talk our way.
When actually a little French,
Will go a long, long way.

We utter a few basics,
Our differences dissolve.
Eloquence can open up,
That Gallic French resolve.

So when in France out walking,
Alone or with your wife.
Say, Bonsoir, messieurs-dame,
You may make friends for life.

WHATSTANDWELL WEIR

On the River Derwent at Merebrook, Whatstandwell, in the Peak District, Derbyshire.

I sit here, atop the salmon ladder,
My legs hang downward.
Cool rejuvenating air rises upward, toward me.
The Derwent flows in a torrent beneath my dangling, suspended feet.

The river rushes with an incessant thunder beneath me,
Assailing and overcoming my senses.
From such a frantic and hateful world
I am conveyed to an enraptured realm of peace and simplicity,
With the entirety of pain frustrated and thwarted in its attempts to
overwhelm me.

The burgeoning roar of the watercourse is audibly penetrated,
By shrill calls and choruses of nearby songbirds,
Granting me the privilege to eavesdrop on their feathered endeavours.

I open my eyes.
Sunlight glints spectacularly
Off the rapidly shape-shifting surface of the main body of water,
Resembling a stellar-studded expanse of cobalt carpet.
It causes me to squint at its radiant intensity.

I transfer my line of vision
To observe the effervescent billowing foam afore me
Form abstract patterns, before finally receding.
Their spuming shapes dissolve and disperse,
Coursing off toward dappled shade.

Not a soul to be seen.
A plethora of variegated greens,
Become a verdant backdrop to my riverside scene.

I am distracted;
The diversion, two begrimed brown cygnets,
Glide in pearlescent elegance.
Their salacious movements a direct juxtaposition
To the riotous cacophony of silence,
Enveloping the churning depths of the Derwent.
I hear nothing but nature.

I am lost but saved by engulfing, bustling, serenity.
Here on my doorstep there is exquisite natural beauty,
Harmony at my home, security and solace in my mind.
Lost in wonder, not lost in life, tranquillity redefined.

Peace and comfort in my mind
Conquers conflict, loss and strife.
Shuts out the false, perverted world,
Gives new meaning to honest life.

WYRLEY HOUSE - (ANTI-SOCIAL HOUSING)
Wyrley House was the location of the murder of Candice Williams in 1978.

This high-rise will never be an apartment block.
Austere with unusable balconies, rusting steel and columns of glass.
Irrespective of any refurb or makeover,
It will forever remain; a block of flats.

Its hard, sharp edged, yet banal concrete soars above scarred tarmac
and superficial splendour.
Thirteen luckless floors of communal isolation.
A characterless monument to human malevolence,
An unconscious host to rape, murder and abjection.

I recall the night-time façade of boxes and windows,
Resembling an elongated crossword puzzle with many blank spaces.
Bleak, thought-provoking, many in darkness,
Those illuminated, remain devoid of human faces.

A bewildering conundrum; anti-social social housing.
A 60's anathema built for the noblest reasons.
A testament to the sheer ordinariness, but unpredictability of life,
And presenting another paradox; freedom in public open prisons.

The lofty parapet scowls down on the hard-hearted facts;
Wyrley House will forever remain; a block of flats.

OUR LUNAR COMPANION

Cherubic face, chromatic pale,
Looks down at us at night.
Glassy at distance, craggy, frigid closer,
Yet, a recurrent romantic sight.

Emerging as we go to bed,
Receding as we all rise.
Inanimate it may undoubtedly be,
But its presence inspires the wise.

It's bold when cold yet coy behind clouds,
Its stature waxes and wanes.
And whilst its being emits no lunar light,
It illuminates darkened lanes.

It entices waves and drives the seas
With immense significant effect.
Missions sent to explore its soul
Disregard deserved respect.

Beyond our natural grasp,
This is another world, a place of visions.
We strive to seize its mystical enchantment,
Exemplification of man's endeavour and conquering ambitions.

An apparent titan midst diminutive gemstones,
An interplanetary illusion with stars about strewn,
The illusion of closeness radiates veneration.
Our intimate, yet very public, ethereal moon.

TWELVE TRUSTED AND TRUE

I sit in the jury waiting room,
One of many twelves, trusted and true.
I people watch my group of peers,
Observe our twelve trusted and true.

One quorum out,
I watch them walk;
Not one smiling; disinclined to talk.
Others wait in excitement, in dread, in hope anew,
Whilst I sit and watch our twelve trusted and true.

We are a random mix.
An abstract, random selection.
Without favour, chosen few.
I watch our twelve trusted and true.

A virtual silence, air-con hums.
Retired, blue-collar workers, professionals, single mums
Sitting impatiently, guarded, apprehensive.
My distraction voyeuristic; I watch the twelve trusted and true.

Many sit in solitude, mobile phone presupposing attention,
Retreating into the comfort of perceived isolation, forestalling tension.
Several flick through dog-eared magazines, attention span askew,
Eyes surreptitiously raised to others; others trusted and true.

One in a corner, dyed blonde, anxious, nervous,
Bitten nails, fearful of her duty, her social service.
Scratching and rubbing, arms a blotchy, ruddy hue,
I watch her, solitary, one of twelve trusted and true.

She stares at floor and feet, picks cotton in strands.
Looks up from knees only to gaze, stare trance-like at her hands.
Unable to make eye contact with me or with you,
I observe panic build inside, this one of our twelve trusted and true.

Released from responsibility, her relief absolute and palpable.
Scarf hiding expression, though her reprieve so visible.
Departs in embarrassed silence, exit hurried too,
Escaping the obligations of twelve trusted and true.

Days become weeks, trials become tribulations.
However, duty is eventually fulfilled, though perhaps not our
expectations.
We leave our enforced dispassionate segregated curfew,
Emerging no longer a member of twelve trusted and true.

ARRIVALS

We shuffled through the arrivals hall.
The sensation was of being in an over-lit aquarium.
Beyond our translucent walled cocoon, lay an out of reach darkness,
Fluorescence merely reflecting the interior and our own insignificance.

Exiting into the night-air countenanced a rush of airiness.
Ethereal moonlight cast dramatic ripples of ineffable beauty.
The clarity and freshness was at odds with the cruelness beyond;
A world of callous construction, severity, glass and steel.

This chromatic radiance created acute line-edged patterns and inky animations,
The embracing coolness, enhanced by shimmering puddles.
Water spiders skated 'cross these diminutive pools,
As if cavorting over the hostile surface of life.

Towering buildings rise like sharp predatory fangs in a screaming mouth of
urban savagery,
Waiting to consume the unsuspecting, the unprepared and the innocent.
Their viciousness inexplicably emphasized by a romantic luminescence;
A pallid illusion of tranquillity, in reality, a gateway to an abyss.

We had forsaken soft worn stone with an undulating and meandering past,
For the malevolence and hardness of concrete, slabs and peoples,
Whose dark and bloody history remains unwelcoming and intimidating.
In essence we had left the harmony and friendship of the Peak District,
And arrived in the turmoil, disorder and sickness that is 'The City'.

NORMAL (I USE THE TERM LOOSELY)

I used to be invincible,
Walked on water, though covered in ice.
Attempted to fly off the roof of a barn,
Aged eight, paid the price.

Young adult years raced cars and bikes,
Yes crashed, but still bounced back.
My resilience indomitable,
Keeping me on track.

When older, indestructible,
Tackled men with guns and knives.
Risked my life, even shot at,
In a world where violence thrives.

Late forties I began to slow,
But immortal felt I remained.
Crashed vehicles to earn a living,
Yet my body rarely complained.

Eventually reached late fifties
A shock for me in store.
My back said "I have had enough,
I can't take any more".

Then my peers, who once surrounded me,
Many began to die.
I was forced to stop, take stock,
Assess, consider "why?".

I managed well 'til sixty,
Then I too fell apart.
A year from hell near' broke me,
My body, my mind, my heart.

But I've since bounced back, recovered,
Learnt the truth, which can be brutal.
I never was invincible
Merely vulnerable, fearful
And, dare I say it, normal.

STARING EYES

A leap of faith
A leap to death
One leap that needed
One final breath

A leap from the twelfth
Into warm soporific air
A leap concluding life
And dousing despair

Those final seconds
What's in their minds?
Presumably not
Those left behind

And me, as I look down
On a waxen faced body
Can only conclude
That those eyes have a story

SADDLEWORTH MOOR

The untainted wild exhilaration can be dark and brooding.
Its stunning, breath-taking landscape
Has a malevolent side; bleak, brutal and punishing.
Raw natural beauty and splendour of isolated remoteness,
Juxtapose a burial ground of hidden openness.

Embraced by the many and chosen by the few,
The Moors' majesty may be tainted by infamy,
But remains essentially innocent, in its unadulterated purity.
The landscape, consumes and overwhelms but makes no judgements,
Waiting only for perspectives and use, to determine viewpoints.

BUTTERFLIES

There are lots of pretty butterflies
That flutter by on the wing.
But really, are they just posh moths
With superficial bling?

Weavers never see a loom,
Red Admirals not go to sea.
There are even Dingy Skippers
And a Duke Of Burgundy.

American Painted Ladies,
You can guess from whence they came.
Gatekeepers and a Hedge Brown
Who share their Latin name.

These delicate wraiths of beauty
Have relatives by the score.
Sub-species and a genus
But of this, I will not bore.

I'll just revel in their appearance,
Their style and grace in flight.
Remarkable in their colours,
Even plain old Cabbage White.

MY BAMBOO BEE

Leaves dither and quiver,
Bees lazily dance
Probing for pollen
Or a queen for romance.

Flitting 'twixt bushes
Close to the ground,
A hole in a stone
Perchance home to be found?

From shrub to bamboo
Movements erratic.
For minutes he flits,
Chaotic, balletic.

Continual searching
Before settling down
In dried vegetation
Leaves crisp, taupe and brown.

Respite only brief,
Off hunting once more,
His golden striped body
Hovers close to the floor.

Then all at once; gone
Floated off on the air,
My buzz of excitement
Gone, I know not where.

HOOPOE

Have you ever seen a hoopoe?
Have you ever even heard,
Of such a brassy, feathered thing
That looks at times, absurd?

It's a throwback from the 80's,
When punk had just occurred,
Yet somewhat more exquisite
With beauty it's conferred.

Black and white topped mohican,
Feathered and not furred.
Caramel fawn, slender neck,
Long beak, sleek and curved.

This punk rock beauty flies with grace
Though somewhat caricatured.
Its singing voice outstanding,
Yet utters not one word.

Monochrome winged from Africa
To Europe summers stirred.
It really is a most resplendent,
Magnificent, exotic bird.

A BROWN BEAR THAT IS GREEN
(Alaska 2007)

Silken smooth verdant jade,
A precious gemstone carved bear.
No more than three centimetres tall and yet,
With indigenous significance beyond compare.

Hand sculpted, fashioned by Navaho peoples,
Delicately detailed, naive without flaws.
A salmon, perhaps once thrashing,
Clasped in deceptively powerful yet exquisitely etched jaws.

This diminutive green beast, for a lifetime to come,
Will undoubtedly gaze across at me with unyielding elegance.
A tactile reminder, with aesthetic simplicity,
Of a supremely wonderful adventure and incredible experience.

RELIGION

Crimson, creeping, congealing blood,
Clagging with desiccated fissured dirt.
Cries of the wounded, moans of the hurt.

This, in the name of religion; never.
No other cheek to turn,
Just beheadings using serrated knives,
And letting innocents suffer or burn.

Auschwitz; perchance a mere blot on the landscape of life,
Though now a place of peace; silent, still, serene.
An exemplification of man's inhumanity to man,
Yet, a lesson not learned, it would seem.

History; littered with mankind's errors, failings and imperfections.
It happened, continues, and forever, still will.
For death and destruction, are for nought,
Being misguided, injudicious and at vilest, a thrill.

Christians, with their murderous crusades,
1200 years before Mumbai-type shootings.
Lorries driven into peaceful, innocent, human beings,
Palmyra style destruction, the killing fields and lootings.

Coptics murdered by Muslims,
Islamists persecuted by all,
Yet all our Gods, without exception,
Reject violence, peace their rallying call.

From Bataclan, Paris to Manchester
They're the scum that stain our Earth;
Murderers and butchers of blameless and children;
Filth attempting, in some perverted way, to justify own worth.

The slaughter of inoffensive, unknowing innocents
Their own religions would not condone.
They are cowardly deranged individuals
Who, together, act alone.

It is the zealots, the unhinged, the twisted,
For whom true religion has lost its tangible meaning.
In a way that benevolent, peace loving people
Find repugnant, sacrilegious, demeaning.

Auschwitz was only more shocking
For the unashamed documentation, meticulously kept.
It continues to resonate within us as a reminder of degraded ideals and beliefs,
Whilst we empathise and sympathise with those for whom we have wept.

In the present, we have social media; Facebook and Twitter
And scrutiny shows slaughter still transpires today.
Al Jazeera and the BBC saturate our minds,
Which merely highlights society has lost its proverbial way.

So please remove from your mind; 'my religion is the right one',
Embrace and accept a true reason for living.
Should we disregard religion? Would this restore peace and harmony?
That panacea of life, for which we are all striving?

I agonise, as for many this may be a step too far, too wrong.
But what I want from life is a ceasefire that is strong.
One that that lasts for ever, not one that's merely long.
A future of peace, recollections in song,
Fundamentally a society, where we simply all get along.
Will this happen? Perhaps, when hell freezes over.

Keith Terry

DOUGHY YES NO!
(K from Kilburn)

Doughy yes no!
This statement refers not to cakes or bread.
It's a lesson in listening to what is being said.
A soggy bottom; nowhere to be seen,
Well, not at the moment, I'll explain what I mean.

I'll go back a little, you'll then understand,
A short time before, a mere wave of the hand.

I've started work as a volunteer,
Transport people where they require to go.
I take their wheelchairs, carers, clamp chairs secure,
Then drive avoiding potholes, carefully, slow.

I pick up K from Kilburn,
He's suspicious, guarded
You could even say troubled.
My new face a change to his routine,
An addition to faces he knows and has seen.

I wheel K to the tail-lift yet,
Even in the constraints of his chair
He tries to shrink away.
Fear palpable, profound, despite what we say.

K shakes and shivers as the snowflakes fall, swirling around us,
Softening our harsh reality.
K complains of the chilling cold
With struggled and slurred verbalisation,
An uncontrolled, unwelcomed sensation.

The tail-lift rises and I wheel K
Into the comparative cocoon-like interior of my bus.
As I clamp his wheelchair to the fastenings in the floor,
Cerebral Palsy clamps his contorted fingers to his own chair handrails,
Protesting once more.

Finally, I ratchet the straps taught, secure and straight,
A direct juxtaposition to K's vulnerable and twisted body.

We set off cautiously to our destination,
An autistic centre where K can vent his frustration.
But during our journey he endeavours to joke
Just like any other bloke, uttering *"Doughy yes no!"*.

His carer looks puzzled, pensive, dismayed,
"I'm sorry K, what did you say?".
Misshapen sneer evident, repetition slow,
A maddened mutter before; *"Doughy yes no"*.

Another perplexed look and she asked again,
K's visage an image of frustration and pain
As he echoes; *"Doughy yes no"*.

Now, K's just like me; a sense of humour twisted,
And an off the cuff quip cannot be resisted.
I relate to K, know what he has jested
And explain his advice with syntax corrected;
Don't eat yellow snow!

SAFETY IN NUMBERS

(This poem was originally conceived in an attempt to try and convey the tension felt on a live police firearms operation. However, like many of my poems, I am inclined to ramble, meander and skew my original intentions.)

Subtle contours under account-purchased jackets
Constricted confines
Pounding temples
Hyped anticipation of the plans
Inane chatter
Awkward silences, and yet;
You cannot hear birds.

Hours of forced waiting for one repeated word
The smell of cordite,
Tension, fear
Surging adrenalin preceding ultimate confrontation
Movements seemingly suspended in time, and yet;
You cannot hear birds.

Glinting, flashing stainless steel
Punctured holes between the ribs
Cadavers drained of life
Lie silently on brushed steel tables, and yet;
You cannot hear birds.

Twisted metal
Twisted limbs
Broken bodies young and old
Intense scrutiny to establish why, and yet;
You cannot hear birds.

The fights
The bottles
The beatings
The visits
Waiting patiently with hope in cubicles, and yet;
You cannot hear birds.

However

No Guns
No knives
No wasted lives
I can hear birds

No blood
No stitches
No screaming bitches
I can hear birds

No hatred
No violence
No vitriolic vengeance
I can hear birds

If I can hear birds I have shed former life,
If I can hear birds I know I am safe.
If I can hear birds it is tranquil and calm.
The birds that I hear protect me from harm.
The more birds I hear the safer I'll be,
There is safety in numbers and salvation for me.

SHOT AT

You have no idea where they come from,
You only hear the sound.
Incredulity becomes realisation,
As bullets strike the ground.

Your sensations and senses heighten,
A swathe of silence descends.
Though adrenalin allows through voices,
On which your life may depend.

Deceptive serenity develops,
Decisions instinctively made.
A relieving sound emerges,
Support through rotary blades.

Procedures intuitively followed,
No rush, you check your friends.
But look forward to the moment,
When the madness finally ends.

Operation carefully concluded,
No-one hurt, other than pride.
Round two will be another day,
But for now; relief inside.

FEAR

Separating lines of opposing fans,
Packaged bombs in discarded cans.
Bottles raining from many sides,
Fronting up to machetes, firearms or knives.

Fights on balconies stories high,
Explaining to families; you don't know why.
The message of death you can never get used to,
Desperate, dying people that reach out to you.

Pursuing headlong into darkness, consequences concealed,
Never walking again, requiring a chair that is wheeled.
Being shot at from buildings high up above,
Is nothing compared to the real fear of
Losing the one you love.

THE TWINS
(Born 2nd October 2018)

Born so small, life so tenuous.
Tiny features, delicate, fragile,
Following a birth, precarious and strenuous.

A short, yet laboriously long journey into the world,
Emphasizing the resilience of new-born life,
Whilst the dangers of delivery slowly unfurled.

No manual, no instructions, only sixth sense and intuition.
Demanding, challenging, stressful and tiring,
But then again rewarding and truly satisfying.

Double the trouble, double the pleasure,
Double the delight that you can treasure.
An ultimate reward;
Memories of love that will last forever.

THE TWINS
(Another twin poem, what a coincidence)

Born small fragile
Life so tenuous
Birth traumatic
Tough and strenuous

No instructions
Draining demanding
Tiring precarious
Satisfying rewarding

Double the trouble
Double the pleasure
Double the delight
You can truly treasure

THE CREMATION OF MORIARTY THE PUNK MACKEREL

Moriarty was stunned, how could this be?
On the day he had decided to quit smoking,
He been captured, pulled from the sea.

Caught hook, line and sinker.
Boxed with mates and packed with ice.
Taken ashore, sold and shipped off, albeit for a good price.

He strove to concentrate, trawled his wits
To escape from what appeared to be an oven,
Full of smoke and apparently, oak chips.

But his eyes, with the heat, glazed over.
His piercings, enflamed and jagged.
His oily complexion fell apart
All in all, he felt gutted.

THE OWL AND THE PUSSYCAT
Renga format. 5-7-5 - 7-7 syllables

The owl and the cat
Went off to sea in a boat
An unlikely pair
In unusual transport
Chosen by whom do you think?

Perchance the feline
Or perhaps the bird of prey
Strange choice for either
Bedfellows extraordinaire
Poetic mariner chums

Folk from a poem
Of Carrollesque concoction
Who are all mad here
Together with a walrus
And carpenter on a beach

An epic in rhyme
Product of a vivid mind
Classic fantasy
A delight for our children
A delectation for life

DUREX TEST DRIVER
(The true story of my 1970 Ford Escort on our wedding day - Sonnet form)

Durex test driver, in foam, adorned the side of our car.
Tin cans rattled their chorus behind.
Off the roof-rack flew knickers, a sight quite bizarre.
Etiquette of honeymoon defined.

Our overnight case swollen, with contents tampered,
Party popper confetti instead.
No underwear found, her lingerie scattered,
What would she wear in bed?

A week in the sun baked the foam on our Ford
As we drove round the Isle of Wight.
A scene for the locals that could not be ignored
A comical yet naughty delight.

The slogan tarnished paintwork, in everlasting embrace.
Like our marriage, until death, unendingly in place.

THE ULTIMATE GIFT

Seemingly inconsequential moments
Mean more to me than ever before.
Material possessions lose all significance.
I look forward to a genuine smile,
Crinkled eyes and tender caress,
Dulcet tones the best redress.

Brittle perhaps weak I may currently be,
Though grow stronger through passage of time.
I appreciate the meaningful points of life,
Such as friendship, trust and openness.
Support from those closest, when in a world of soup
Armed only with a fork and trying to regroup.

Caring and compassion proliferate happiness,
Altruism transmits peace and contentment,
Whilst materialism and avarice breed anger, resentment.
The ultimate gift in life, we learn;
Is the gift of loving and being loved in return.

ADVICE TO YOUR CHILDREN

Find your own voice
And comprehend its worth
Speak your own words
Not the oaths of others

Ask the questions of life
That you want answered
Not the questions
Others expect you to ask

Take steps in your life
Along the paths you wish to tread
Not in the directions
Others would wish you to follow

Look at life with values
That you hold dear
Not with the tainted views
Others may hold

Wish and strive for what you
Want to achieve in life
Not for what others
May materialistically expect you to desire

Be at peace and content with yourself
And with the world
Do not kowtow and fall in line
With the greed of others

Understand the needs of others
And not what others may just want
Be selfless and appreciate;
You do not necessarily come first
And that giving is invariably receiving

Beyond all be yourself
And be proud to be your own self
For life is all about understanding
Who we are and what we will be

Remember;
Keeping an open and honest mind
Is an interminable, never-ending process
Concluding only
When we have drawn
Our last breath

HONESTY IS NOT AN OPTION

Hearing the truth can be frightening
Being open means having to be brave
Honesty is not an option
It is compulsory
And with it brings realisation
An understanding of how far I have come
But also recognition
Of how far I have still to go

Fear for my future is now circumvented
Challenged by anticipation and knowledge
Of what is still to come
And what I have yet to achieve

The darkness of mortality
Is more than counterbalanced
By love, friendship and support,
Adventures, journeys and encounters
Discoveries to be made
Stories to be told
A bright future to unfold

HAPPY ENDING?

Happy content
Little to repent
Friendships valued
Forever continued

Worried scared
Perhaps ill prepared
Lucky and faithful
Loved and thankful
For a journey shared

Future doubting
Strength concerning
Togetherness to solitary
Happiness to tragedy
Inevitability the ending

PARENTS

Always there, always true.
Always supportive,
No matter what we do.

Watch our lives as we live.
Always listen
And ready to forgive.

Trust and rely on them,
Remaining calm,
Never rush to condemn.

Toiling days, sleepless nights,
To give us wings,
Prepare us for flight.

With instinct, kept from astray,
Without instructions,
Helped us find our way.

Greatest gift, love and time.
We give our thanks,
You gave us a lifetime.

FINALITY BITES

Confused
Vulnerable
Tragic
Old

Fretful
Frightened
Overheated
Cold

Restless
Dispirited
Tired
Trying

Depressed
Distressed
Desperate
Dying

WIND

Wind is a strange phenomenon.
How does it start? Why is it there?
Why is it here and also elsewhere?
For something that is colourless,
Why does it fade, having caused such mess?

Wind makes no sound, so noisily.
It wends its way through tops of trees,
A rushing sound when a stronger breeze.
So quiet when cooling, loud when cold,
Refreshing when young, biting when old.

Wind is invisible, cannot be seen.
Branches sway, flags on masts,
We watch the wind as it races past.
When gentle, dancing leaves leave smiles,
When harsh, destruction viewed for miles.

Wind has no elemental being.
It does not exist, yet has a scale.
Its harnessed strength is used for sail.
It has no size, no light to emit.
I ponder on wind. Oh what is it?

WINDSDAY

"It's Windsday", he cried,
Breaking Milne's copyright,
But the clouds drift by quickly,
Confirming he's right.

The shutters rattled,
The trees waved their arms.
The birds flew for cover
Chirping alarms.

Silently morphing,
Clouds racing by.
White fluffy pillows
'Cross Wedgwood blue sky.

Leaves blew through the terrace,
Pine needles too.
Spiders clung tightly
As Windsday blew.

Then all of a sudden
Just as it started,
A hush descended
And Windsday departed.

It ended with a whisper,
Having given its shout.
Poor old Windsday
Had blown itself out.

MEMORIES

Memories are such an enigma.
Recollections of past times gone by.
There are moments we strive to forget
but fail, notwithstanding, we try.

Some instants held in our memory,
become twisted, distorted from truth.
Others are recalled like blueprints
from events way back in our youth.

There are times we'd love to remember,
to recount for the rest of our days.
The trouble with memory is old age,
times more of a blur or a haze.

Memories may fade or stay pin sharp,
but no matter what others may say,
remember those moments of magic,
for no-one can take them away.

A WORRYING MEMORABLE EXPERIENCE

As I progress toward my impending old age
I comprehend my memory is not what it used to be.
I realise that much of my forgetfulness
Is neglecting to see what I see.

I frequently fail to concentrate,
Assimilate information acquired through my ears.
It gets lost amongst the workings of my mind
Gets muxed ip or disappears.

I worry that in the looming future
My memory may metamorphose to dementia.
Yet realise; worrying over whether I will lose my memory,
Is itself an ingredient of dilemma.

I often focus to exaggerated extreme
On matters unimportant or trivial.
Feel impatient when there is no rush,
When deferment is more judicial.

Experience tells me there'll be a problem.
Experience tells me agonizing over it is, in itself, strife.
Experience tells me worrying about something I have no
control over is futile.
Experience tells me that experience is the bane of one's life.

LIQUORICE TOFFEE WRAPPERS

Tom trundled toward the allotments
Though no longer toiled his plot
Patch now tended by perceived youth
Following illness engendered absence

His scooter sails silently along shingle trail
Mangy flea-infested pooch lopes alongside
Twice daily sojourns a reason for living
A routine repeated without fail

Evidence of devotion; discarded wrappers
Liquorice toffees an involuntary ritual
Cast off consciously though unavoidably
Dealt with empathetically by imposed receivers

Fine silt grit pathway now devoid of testimony
No paw prints litter or tracks
No collection of purple silver wraps
And a wheelchair left discharged
An attestation of a concluding determining destiny

LIBERATION

Blood, the essence of life, rushes through my veins.
Thoughts, the cause of strife, race around my brain.
Sporadic waves of visceral emotions wash over me.
Temples pound, body joints racked with inexplicable pain.

Diazepam drowsiness dulls illogical sensations.
Comfort is reaped from nature and its untainted distractions.
Solace and peace achieved as mental traumas disappear,
Watching birds and creatures with their purposeful actions.

Neurotic forgetfulness adds to tension and fears.
Convulsions and saltiness from irrepressible tears
Impose their skewed reality which I endeavour to assuage.
Life and death's harsh realities offend and violate my ears.

Osprey-like talons grasp at my existence and enrage,
Drawing me in, absorbed but unwilling captive in my psychological cage.
Temporary intermissions become hesitations, a mere intervener.
But I am luckier than most, soon to be free to re-engage.

I wait, though time passes slowly, I will not be a figurative prisoner,
Liberation merely around a metaphorical corner.
I am supported by a rallying team, a family close and wider.
I am conscious that I am not, and never will be, a loner.

WHAT KIND OF PERSON?

What kind of person takes a life
To satiate their own desire?
Rips apart families, affects all involved,
Causing immense pain like a rapacious vampire?

What kind of person murders for thrill,
Is aroused by ultimate control?
Has no conscience of consequence,
Thinks only of self and not of the whole?

What kind of person rapes without qualm,
Destroys a life, and that of others?
One without ethics or morals,
Leaving lives irrevocably altered?

What kind of person does all this without care?
One without scruples, perchance a psychopath?
Deranged, unhinged and dangerous,
Oblivious and indifferent of society's wrath?

Is this a person we should seek to help?
Should we eliminate them, or keep them in prison?
Are they a perpetrator to hate or pity?
An offender to be terminated or one to be forgiven?

This is society's choice, collectively yours and mine.
Subsequently we all have to live with the consequences;
And remember, that once that choice is made,
The reverberations and ramifications are on our consciences.

PROBLEMS, WHAT PROBLEMS?

We moan about our problems,
but are they such a chore?
We fix things then get on with life,
though still we whinge some more.

Let's put things in perspective,
some problems just aren't so.
They open up new avenues,
on the route of life we go.

When you hear of real problems
that others have in life,
ours pale to insignificance,
mere adventures, with some strife.

There is death and war and famine
and where freedom is curtailed.
Yet all we seem concerned about
is why our shares have failed.

Whilst friends lose family members
and fight off Death's disease,
We should realise we're lucky,
our life's comparatively a breeze.

So when you have a burst pipe,
or a car that will not start,
remember those less fortunate
and reach out with your heart.

THANK YOU

Our tarnished society wakes to a new realisation.
The few outweigh the wishes of a vast majority.
They impact on those of us who wish for peace.
Our outrage is the recognition of this minority.

Unprepared to accept responsibility,
Always willing to blame others for their acts.
Behaviour that erodes self-discipline,
The fault never theirs, as they riot in packs.

Excuses paraded for media.
Lack of work? Nothing to do and bored?
Knowing the state will bail them out,
Lazy lie-in mornings from drink or having scored.

Schools without discipline, reward without effort,
The excused bad behaviour termed expression.
Crimes without punishment, balance not redressed,
All sides dysphoric with depression.

Easy success paraded for precious little work,
Instant fame the effortless panacea.
No one fails, we have deferred success,
Retakes and resubmissions in academia.

De-moralised or just demoralised?
The moral maze of our welfare systems.
We must address the causes,
Repair and dissect the symptoms.

Let's start at the roots; with attitudes,
Respect, manners and motivation.
Thank you – phrase simple, words few,
Yet behind them, appreciation.

I'M JUST A DOWNTRODDEN SOD

I start to grow but am downtrodden, depressed,
I'm shit on and peed on by those who know best.
I start to mature, but get cut down to size,
Continual development becomes my demise.

I'm rolled on and lain on, often covered and die,
Yet you care for me, love me, and I do not know why.
I live close to my neighbours, in fact tightly packed,
Bond great in a group, and that is a fact.

I live for all sports, from football to cricket.
Have hurling, horse racing and golf to my credit.
Tennis, lacrosse, rugby and polo,
Requested by teams as well as for solo.

So if I'm so popular and in such demand
Why am I trodden on, by all in the land?
Is it because I've a blade, I'm a pain in the ass?
No;
It's just me and my mates are a field made of grass.

A MARS A DAY HELPS YOU WORK, REST AND WRITE SILLY POEMS

A Mars a day helps
You work, rest and play,
The advert on TV,
To music, did say.

It's odd looking back,
I just cannot recall.
Ever eating chocolate
to rest at all.

And chocolate for hard work?
Well it gives you a kick,
But half an hour later,
You're just left feeling sick.

I fancy them often,
But rarely indulge.
Just thinking of calories
Makes my tummy bulge.

Bacon when camping
Is similar in vein.
Smells out of this world,
Tastes not quite the same.

Mars, you think "Oh yes",
Unwrap it so quick.
Yet as soon as you've scoffed it
You're thinking, "That's it?"

So sorry Mars UK
I try not to decry,
Or interrupt sales
Of what consumers may buy.

I'm just getting older,
Fussier too.
So I won't have a Mars bar,
I'll have to have two!

WAITING WORDS

The words lie hidden, trapped between hard impermeable covers.
Weaved into text, line twixt line, waiting to be read,
Waiting to be discovered.

They wait patiently, quietly unspoken, unable to deliver.
Remote and forlorn in compiled isolation, alone with little meaning.
But optimistically not forever.

Words emerge from their embryonic form,
When given life with our breath.
Their communal existence given potency and significance,
Conveying everything from birth, through life and death.

Dormant on pages, entombed in a tome,
A sentence of confinement in their literary home.
Unopened, trapped and in monochrome,
Yet words can make all the difference.

With pace; enhanced excitement,
With research; insight and enlightenment.
Blend love with contentment,
Words make all the difference.

Pupae to chrysalis then birth of butterflies,
Interwoven plots can twist truths to lies,
Explain and help us realise,
Those words make all the difference.

The inconsequential expands to life-changing prose.
Banal lifted to extraordinary, the hidden; exposed.
From imprisoned to open, knowledge disclosed.
Yes; words can make all the difference.

PETANQUE

2013 saw an International pétanque tournament held at Montalivet in the Southwest of France, with individuals and teams from around the world. I'm afraid England did not fare too well, but whilst spectating I did think...

Pétanque, a strangely sounding game,
Like bowls but slightly different rules.
The bowl metallic, not of wood,
In fact not bowls at all, but boules.

Silver alloy boules that clack
As opponents boules are struck.
And unlike bowls, the boules aren't rolled,
It's more a stylish chuck.

The closest boules, achieve the scores,
Quite simple it would seem.
The duel, exchange, continuing,
Until someone's reached thirteen.

You could score one for closest boule,
Double for closest two.
If competitors are closely matched
Then ends, there are a few.

Now I've said "end", but that's not the end,
It's really just one part.
The 'ends' then add together,
Each taking turns to start.

Theses boules, each person, they have three,
But what order? That's not set.
It depends upon the distance,
Who's the closest they can get.

"But close to what?" I hear you ask.
Oops, I'd best explain.
There's a smaller ball, let's call him Jack,
He's the target in the game.

On reflection, for a simple sport,
I give complex description,
And rather than some easy prose,
I've commenced a work of fiction.

Perhaps the ideal answer is
Those Gallic skills to see.
Learn procedures from the side-lines,
Not work out the rules from me.

THREE SPEED GARDEN
Written in a few minutes looking out of our patio doors at the trees in our garden

The branches of the buddleia bounced beautifully in the wind
Its pink-tipped fronds languidly stroking the air like an artist's bristles
Lacking only a fabric canvas

Alongside; russet red leaves of a Canadian maple dance jauntily
Their pace seemingly at odds with the languid strokes of its cerise festooned neighbour
Its long-limbed petioles clinging tightly to sturdy stalks

In contrast; bamboo foliage is busy bustling in a forced frenzy
Movement of the slim leaves frenetic and urgent yet almost imperceptible
Its dithering agitations tiny and restricted

Random voluminous abstract patterned clouds race across the skies
The monochromatic moody morphing shapes drift nomadically from sight
In a colossal soundless shifting struggle

I sit in my double-glazed bubble mesmerised and captivated
Enlivened by the natural chaos bustle and commotion beyond my balcony
All a contradiction to the serene stillness and calm equanimity of my lounge

Sunlight suddenly erupts through the dull and drab morning
But almost immediately, swiftly softens, fading into insignificance
As battle between dawn and billowing clouds rages beyond my window

This mammoth melee occurs in a cacophony of silence
I sit cocooned in quiet contemplative comfort
Peace broken only by the staccato ticking of time above me

Finally this enchantment is enhanced
Heart-warming sunshine gloriously and unashamedly proclaims
Its triumphant energising presence

However; an exceedingly unexpected resonance
Suddenly cuts through my moment of rapturous enthrallment
"The shower's free!"

THE FAMILY ROOM

During thirty seven years I made countless visits to family/relatives rooms of numerous hospitals whilst on duty. In June 2015 the tables were turned and it was my turn to be on the receiving end, when I was left in the family room to wait for news.

The family room; an enigma ill-defined
A room relatively misnamed
A room for compassion, for kinship
Togetherness proclaimed

That hospital room; a misnomer
Antonym to all we hold dear
A place of doubts, of grief, of loss,
Concern, anxiety, fear

Ascetic, stark and practical
Sofas a nod to only perceived comfort
Devoid of hope and personality
Veiled privacy becomes abandonment

A place perhaps my nemesis
A curse throughout my life
A place breeding sadness and passing
The antithesis of full family life

THE JOURNEY (A POLITE TITLE)

The toilet gurgled with relief
as its contents started their journey to the sewage beds.
Tumbling almost silently along dark, earthen bowels
before being disgorged into misty, murky open sheds.

Dank and sepia, the waves of stench arise
fighting for dominance with fresh country air.
The sea of fetid remains lay discarded
like unwanted carcasses in a dragon's lair.

The battle between light and dark rages
with an unscripted future to unfold.
The highs and lows of trials and endeavour
from conception to conclusion will in the end be told.

The journey may be short in its overall concept,
So enjoy the ride and fear not life's vagaries.
Just remember, in the grand scheme, nothing changes,
it's only the depth that varies.

THE SMOKING CHAV

This poem was motivated by watching a 'chav' quaffing copious amounts of
white wine and, despite being near nine months pregnant, getting slowly
inebriated and smoking like a trooper at a wedding I attended.
The wedding was marvellous, my fears for the baby's future, which may
possibly be unjustified, almost incomprehensible.

Darwin had a theory: the fittest will survive,
The weak fall by the wayside, the resilient stay alive.
Though cruel at times, this truth is tough, the facts of life dictate,
The fittest, strongest, cleverest, invariably acquire their mate.

Intelligent genes evolve, survive, and those that can, adapt.
It's been like that for millennia, a very well-known fact.

But Darwin's theory challenged, subverted more by stealth,
By continual government meddling, which has more to do with wealth.
To keep the punters happy (or protect MPs' grandeur),
They plan to support the needy, and we all agree for sure.

We want to help, that's natural, we're happy to be levied,
To ensure that those with problems, are helped, and never harried.

But our system's become perverted; it encourages the weak.
Rewards the lax who stay at home, so jobs they never seek.
"Why go to work?" they say with pride, "we have our council flats",
Plasmas, laptops, numerous kids, they stay and breed like rats.

Some folk work hard, get nothing, perhaps struggle to conceive,
Whilst others stagnate, shy of work, and pop kids out like peas.

The system then supports them, inspires their idle week.
The hard-working, strong, get obstacles, their future looking bleak.
They smoke whilst they are pregnant, even though they know the score,
But if damage found upon the birth, blame others, then claim more.

If families grow, no problem, they'll be given a bigger home,
But scrimp and save for your own new house, feel abandoned, ignored, alone.

The future for this country is not all bad, I'm sure.
It just seems that at this moment, our priorities are obscure.
We need an instilled ethic, to want to contribute.
To care, support and sympathise, to avoid our own Beirut.

I perhaps view life too simply, overlook the grander scale,
And hopefully there's a solution, true society will prevail.

I know it's wrong to generalise, there are many with genuine need.
There are even those who work too hard, I assume that is agreed.
I do not know the answer; I'm really not that smart.
I just want us all to get along; I mean that from my heart.

So perhaps you will forgive me, for observations skewed by drink.
This poem's just my jaundiced view, perhaps written to make you think.

Keith Terry

PLAYING WITH POEM SHAPES
(Acrostic)

AUTUMN'S GLORIES

Autumn is toiling, preparing and purgin**g**
Unclaimed golden leaves wither and fal**l**
Twirling slowly downwards seemingly s**o**
Unloved, spurned and wasted. Though fo**r**
Many, they become part of that spectacle **I**
Never tire in seeing. The gilded elaborat**e**
Scattering carpets of delight and joyfulnes**s**

FIREWORKS AND SPARKLERS

Fireworks astonish us on Guy Fawkes night**s**
I love the sight of rockets as they shoot u**p**
Racing skywards to a rapturous euphori**a**
Exploding in impressive sounds and colou**r**
We watch in spirited amazement and loo**k**
On towards the heavenly night skies, al**l**
Romantically illuminated with flare and fir**e**
Keeping us transfixed in awe. The sparkle**r**
Seemingly so quiet, if waved before our eye**s**

ShapES

A
circle
is round, I
wonder why so.
A diamond of a
question, yet
round we
go
!

My circle
may seem more
of a diamond, but these shape
patterns are so incredibly hard.
I change syntax to weave out
a pattern. Remembering
there are no rules
in poetry.

A
triangle
is undoubtedly
an interesting shape
with highs and
and its lows,
a point to
make
¥

Squares are so boring
Just regular and plain
We like to see shapes
Differ now and again.

Something that is
curvy,
More comfort than
for speed.
These shapes are exciting
and sexy,
Especially when
You read.

THE COEFFICIENT OF LINEAR EXPANSION IS DEFINED AS: THE FRACTIONAL INCREASE IN LENGTH PER DEGREE RISE IN TEMPERATURE

The coefficient, as set out,
A complex formulae,
Yet somehow well remembered
By a memory-challenged me.

I was taught it in the fourth year
At 15 years of age.
It served no purpose to me then
and thought never will again.

I failed my physics miserably,
'A' level maths also.
So what, I'll never use those things,
Little did I know.

Some 20 years they passed me by
And then, right out the blue,
I needed that old formula,
Plus Newton's motions too.

Tucked away in memory banks
Ready for instant use,
Together with some technical stuff
Of angles all obtuse.

So how do I recall it plain,
Recite it clear as day,
When I can't remember password codes
Set only yesterday?

LE TOUQUET

Ribbons of pasta in a mushroom cream sauce
Coalescing with gésiers, topped with fois gras.
Red Bordeaux from the Gironde's left bank,
And a smile.
The smile that eases
The smile that teases,
A smile that comforts
A smile that pleases.
A leisurely stroll to aid digestion,
Followed by Ricard and an innocent question.

WOMEN

Give a woman a lemon and receive lemonade,
present bitter gourd, fragrant table is laid.
Confront her with crisis and calm is restored,
war becomes dialogue; solutions explored.

Once given a fact, in her memory forever
and when problems are yours, support you with fervour.
Confused with the details? A plan can be made,
Use feminine logic, trust always conveyed.

She contributes so much, she changes her roll,
and in times of panic, retains her control.
She'll assist and provide, her challenges met,
she's defended and nurtured since creation's onset.

Give her a child and she'll make him a man,
to develop her offspring, the best way she can.
Give her a man and she'll make him a whole.
Take the woman away and he loses his soul.

WHAT DO YOU SEEK IN LIFE?

What do you seek in life?
Is it health, is it wealth?
Is it pleasure or peace?
Is it love or is it calm
To walk arm in arm?

Is it comfort or excitement,
Exhilaration or contentment?
Is it to please or purely to live?
Is it to be free,
Or is it to forgive?

Is it to seek or perhaps to find,
To search for inner peace of mind?
Is it for now or for the beyond,
Or is that an illusion, duped all along?

Is it a deception or must we trust?
Is there a truth and is that truth just?
Is it to improve or is it to survive?
Can it be enough to simply be alive?

Is it to understand or solely to see?
I cannot comprehend, for I am merely me.

THE CLOCK

I lie on the settee.
My makeshift bed upholstered in fading worn linen,
Thinning like a schoolboy's elbows.

Hung alongside a cheap framed print of a city scene,
The gilt imitation jewelled wall-mounted clock
Ticks, ebbs and eats away at a lifetime.

The clock resides prominent and stately on a 60's brick façade.
Prepared to be audibly invisible during the woken hours yet
Vocal, vociferous and outspoken whilst those within its reach, sleep.

Capo de Monte figurines sit as if bookends of life,
Embellishing the mantelpiece above a fake-coal fireplace;
The clock ticks.

Toward the window, imitation fabric flowers faded by sunlight
Stand stooped in an anonymous glass vase.
Dawn's sunrise regales with little success
In its encounter with leaden blanket skies
And heavens heavy with pending doom.

Beyond the diamond lead-panelled glass, the world stirs.
Chattering muffled tones of a cold damp motor car
Coughing in its own struggle for life.
A passing freight train trundles behind a row of brick-built cages.
The clock, momentarily overpowered, resumes its metronomic beat.

Another train, another car.
Workers escaping their terracotta tiled prisons
In exchange for labours, perceived enrichment and freedom.
Closer, the chronographic sound pulses in my head.
Its rhythm hammering in the cacophony of silence.

Eventually in the adjacent room, the creaking of a bed.
Sonorous sighs and stirrings from slumber
Announce another day will ensue.
Living, though not a life, continues for another day.

The clock beats with a waning, weakening voice.
Its repetitive tone eventually lost
Amidst desperate, distressed, pleading calls and panic.

I look forward to my own clock,
Companionable silence, shared breathing,
And the comforting resonance of redemption.
I arise from the settee.

THE GRAPES OF WRATH

Pulitzer Prize-winning dramatic film
Directed by John Ford.
But for many folk, that title
Entails an awful lot more.

The Grapes of Wrath, with venom
Pile on unseen pain not pleasure.
Released from inner basement depths
Due to overexerted endeavour.

Haemorrhoids cling and hang
From the bottom of your world,
Now external, tumescent, distended,
Pushed out and part unfurled.

The doctor; so embarrassing,
Yet he's seen it all before.
But not from my perspective
With my trousers on the floor.

Anusol and Germoloids
I'm told will sooth the pain.
Plus raisins, grapes and oranges
So in future, need not strain.

Bath-time is so soothing,
I could soak away for hours.
Relaxing with drink and candlelight
And the fragrance of wild flowers.

Now I realise the painful truth
Despite the sniggers and the smiles.
There is nothing more uncomfortable
Than bulging, itchy piles.

SCARTHIN BOOKS

The Promenade, Cromford, Matlock;
The home of Scarthin bookshop.
Beside a picturesque village pond,
A stunning Peak District backdrop.

The approach a true elevation,
Spirits, mood, perhaps perception.
Well-being, welfare, vigour and tone,
Enhanced by friendly reception.

On entry, or even just passing,
A sense of revelation rises.
For behind the walls of this special place
Are wonders, curiosities, surprises.

It isn't just the assemblage of books,
There're moving walls, endless rooms and cake.
It augments the soul and the psyche,
From merely being awake.

Scarthin Books; a bookshop?
A title so laughably trivial.
A philosophy, a journey, a foray, a must,
A consummate, unparalleled pinnacle.

OH TO BE A CLOUD

Oh to be a cloud
Floating in the blue
Corpulent yet light and white
Enhancing the view for you

Morphing drifting malleable
Continually changing shape
Challenging your mind
As to what pictures you can make

Elephants or puppy dogs
Whose ears rise and fall
Cartoon faces or kitten cats
Toying with a ball

Try not obscuring the sunshine
So you stay warm within
Let the rays of my love and happiness
Gently caress your skin

HAIKUS (5-7-5)

Toffee wrappers

Old Tom gave me sweets
No more discarded wrappers
Wheelchair left discharged

Whatstandwell

Whatstandwell's wide weir
A ladder for the salmon
A haven for trout

The owl and the pussycat

Owl and pussycat
Classic Carrolesque sailors
Such unlikely friends

Jayne with a 'Y'
Haiku & Renga (5-7-5 + 7-7)

She listened, I spoke
Jayne with a 'y' saved my life
She knew my anguish

Lost lids replaced on boxes
Merely a supportive hinge

MY FIRST ONE

Reprised from the original 'Debris Inside My Mind', The poem that started my poetic journey.

Candice was my first one, back in nineteen seventy eight,
Found murdered in a stairwell, in the flats on an estate.

They sent me there, that fateful day, to preserve the primary scene,
Make sure no-one left the block, if returning, where they'd been.

I looked upon her body, the subject of a rape,
As she lay there on that cold hard floor, out of place, behind the tape.

Her Afro hair, her dark brown skin, walls so stark and white,
Contrast sharp and so austere, it did not seem quite right.

The picture of her lying there, position almost foetal,
Life extinguished far too soon, in a manner far too brutal.

I saw me on the news that night, my parents oh so proud,
But I bowed my head and cried again, I'm a bloke, that's not allowed.

Funeral delayed, parents distraught, a family ripped apart.
And others, like ripples on a pond, a list too long to start.

In life I never knew her; we had never even met,
In death our encounter was so short, but Candice I can't forget

Over my time I've seen some shit; bodies, blood and gore,
During thirty years I've seen too much, I pray to see no more.

Of course there were many others, lives taken or defiled,
Yet it's the image of Candice seared in my mind,
For she was my first dead child.

ABOUT THE AUTHOR

Keith Terry was born in 1955 and now lives in Derbyshire's beautiful Peak District.

Keith has been married for over 40 years to a retired teacher and professional musician. They have two children and two grandchildren.

Keith is a former police officer with a 37 year long exemplary career, during which time he has performed duties in a variety of roles from plain clothes to traffic. Whilst on traffic Keith spent nearly 10 years attending, investigating and reconstructing serious and fatal collisions.

His service has diversified from walking the beat and pushing a Panda car around the inner city estates of Birmingham to VIP protection duties in London. He also conducted and assisted in planning anti-terrorist operations and VIP and Royalty protection operations.

The final nine years of his service were spent instructing blue light response and pursuit driving alongside VIP escort anti-terrorist driving techniques, before retiring with a back injury.

During his service he has seen, in his words, "too much shit and gore". This somewhat dark side and skewed view of life is reflected in his poetry.

Keith 'discovered' poetry by sheer luck and this is a story in itself. He has found writing poetry cathartic and stress relieving, after many years of nightmares caused by the traumatic events he has witnessed.

Keith realised putting his fears into words is very psychotherapeutic. Having set down his thoughts on paper, the nightmares have now ceased.

Many of these poems were conceived and written at his bolt hole in the Gironde region of Southwest France. Others were perhaps written at Montalivet for no other reason than he just happened to be there, and it is such an inspiring and relaxing place.

Keith makes no apology for this small book of poems having, perhaps, a slight Gallic bias.

Printed in Poland
by Amazon Fulfillment
Poland Sp. z o.o., Wrocław